CW00860114

What Happened

to

Prince Charming?

Ten Tips To Achieve
a Happy Marriage Life
and Live Happily Ever After

Dana Rongione

What Happened to Prince Charming?

Ten Tips To Achieve a Happy Marriage Life and Live Happily Ever After

Dana Rongione

Published by
A Word Fitly Spoken Press

All Scripture notations are taken from
The Holy Bible, KJV

Table of Contents

Love at first sight is easy to understand;
it's when two people have been looking
at each other for a lifetime that it
becomes a miracle.

Sam
Levenson

Introduction

Once upon a time, there lived a lovely young girl who found herself a prince. The prince was kind and caring. He showed her great love and always put the girl's needs before his own. In all the land, there was no other prince so gallant and brave, loyal and trustworthy, and the girl considered herself blessed beyond her wildest imagination when the handsome prince asked her to marry him.

The wedding was a beautiful affair, and for a while, life with her prince was everything the fair maiden had dreamed of. But, as we know, every good story has trouble, and so it was for the young couple.

Times grew difficult, and the girl found herself wishing for something more, something better. Before long, she began to notice that her handsome prince was changing. No longer was he as selfless and kind as he had been before. As time progressed, the prince began to portray more and more irritating characteristics that baffled and frustrated our young maiden, often leaving the young girl to wonder, "Whatever happened to my Prince Charming? This is not the same man I married."

Perhaps you've heard this tale. Or, worse yet, perhaps you're living it. You are the young maiden who married a Prince Charming that no longer seems to exist. What happened to him? When did he change so much? Why didn't you see this coming? In the coming chapters, I want to answer those questions and many more, but first, allow me to share my own story.

My husband and I met at Bible college and were married in the summer following our second year of school. For the next several months, we both worked full-time jobs during the day and went to school full time in the evenings. We didn't see each other much, and when we did, we were both too exhausted to really spend time together. A day lounging on the couch in front of the television was our idea of Heaven on Earth. Fortunately for us, we were still newlyweds, so the excitement and passion of our first months together kept us firmly in the grip of love and devotion. Little did we know that we were about to face something that would test our promise to love one another for richer or for poorer, in sickness and in health.

Eight months after we were married, I was diagnosed with a severe case of mono. The doctor's prescription was four-fold and hard to swallow—(1) Get lots of rest; (2) Quit your job; (3) Quit school; (4) Don't lift anything heavier than a spoon for at least the next three months. Are you kidding me? How was I supposed to do that? Honestly, I never imagined anyone could feel so bad. I was totally exhausted. My head ached all the time. My glands were swollen to the point that swallowing, yawning, and even talking were a challenge. And because of the severity of the disease, my organs were swollen, resulting in extreme abdominal pain. In short, I was miserable.

Following most of the doctor's advice, I quit my job, spent my days resting and doing as little as possible, and went to school in the evening. I couldn't bring myself to drop out of college because I feared that I wouldn't go back, so though it was difficult and my grades dropped significantly, I continued on. But at that point, we lost our second income, took on a boatload of doctor bills, and found out just how great an impact sickness could have on a marriage.

Fast forward nearly eighteen years to the present. I am still fighting a myriad of physical issues, some of which are a direct result of the mono. I did go back to teaching after I graduated from college, but nine years later, God called me away from that and into the ministry of writing. Two months after I walked away from my job and its income, my husband was fired from his job, leaving us with no income at all. Fortunately, he found another job in little time, but overall, our income was cut in half. Not even two years after that, he was laid off and spent seven months looking for another job. Seven months without a steady income. Seven months of fear and insecurity breathing down our necks every hour of every day. I wish I could say that we were walking by faith, but I think it would be more accurate to say that we were stumbling by faith.

Why am I telling you all of this? Because I want you to understand something very important before we go any further. Some marriages crumble because of one devastating event such as the loss of a child, an affair, or a debilitating illness. The blow to the relationship is so traumatic and severe that the couple sees no recourse other than divorce. More often than not, however, marriages die a "death by a thousand cuts." In ancient China, prisoners were often tied to a wooden frame and subjected to a slow, drawn-out form of torture and execution known as *lingchi*, which means death by a thousand cuts. True to its name, the officials would administer one cut after another to the prisoner's body. Some cuts were long and deep while others were mere pricks. None of them, however, were mortal wounds. The point was to make the prisoner suffer as long as possible while slowly allowing him to bleed to death. Gruesome, I know, but that's exactly what's taking place in most marriages today.

Praise the Lord, many of us have not faced that "one devastating blow" to our married lives. That's not to say, though, that our marriages are not in danger. It's all the "little cuts" that we have to be careful of. Cuts like financial distress, health issues, job frustrations, job loss, children who have gone astray, and on and on the list could go. You know what I'm talking about. It seems as if life just throws one thing after another at you, and you feel as if you're drowning in a sea of confusion and despair. These trials can lead to turmoil and even bitterness between a husband and wife, and most of the time, it's not that they're angry with one another. It's simply that they're angry at life, and they take that anger out on each other. After all, we tend to confide in those we feel the closest to, so it's only natural for us to express our feelings (whether good or bad) to our spouse. Unfortunately, the continual spewing of frustration can create a strain on the marriage, and that is the biggest issue I wish to address throughout this book.

For the purpose of this study, I am going to make some stereotypical statements. What that means is that there may be some things that apply to you and your husband and some things that don't. That's fine. For example, in many instances, the husband tends to be the procrastinator in the family. That may be true in your case, or you may be the one who puts off until tomorrow those things that could be done today. In that case, when you get to the portion where I talk about the procrastinating husband, you can either skip to the next part or read it and get what you can from it. It's up to you. I just want you to understand that I'm not saying that every man is *this* way and every woman is *that* way. Got it?

Okay, now, let's deal with the biggest question on your mind right now—the reason you're reading this book: What happened to your Prince Charming? I have the answer. Are you ready? LIFE! Yep, that's the answer: life happened to him. Think about it, life (with all of its twists and turns) changes us. In some ways, we grow stronger and more confident. In other ways, we become weaker and more dependent on others. We grow. We mature. We change, sometimes for the good and sometimes not. And here's another point that we often fail to think about: life and time affect how close we feel to one another. For example, that seven-month stretch when my husband was out of work was the most precious time in our relationship that I've ever known. Despite the stress and strain of our circumstances, we spent countless hours together during that time and even took up a new hobby of hiking—a hobby that we love and continue today. That event changed us, both individually and as a couple. Life happens, and it will change your husband.

But guess what, ladies? You've changed too. Perhaps just as you're wondering what happened to your Prince Charming, your dear husband is wondering what happened to his fair maiden. Take a few minutes to think back to the way you were when you first met the love of your life. How have you changed since that time? I'm not just talking about physically (Heaven knows, some of us don't even want to go there), but in every respect of our lives. Are you more or less cheerful than you used to be? Do you spend more or less time with your hubby than you used to? Are there things you used to do to show your love that you no longer do? Seriously think about it for a few minutes and take note of the events or circumstances in your life—both good and bad—that have molded you into what you are now.

That being said, I need you to understand that this is not a book about bashing men and their lazy ways. We are not going to blame them for all our troubles and pretend that we have no blame when it comes to our marriage struggles. I think we all know that's not true (and if you don't, then this might not be the right book for you). Do our husbands have faults? Absolutely, we all do. But that's not what I want to focus on. Instead, I want to delve into the issue of how we, as Godly wives, deal with those faults and the negative feelings that spring up out of nowhere when our husbands are getting on our nerves. I want to focus on us, ladies, and our issues. So, if you're ready, dive on in. Yes, the water may be a little icy at first, but if you're truly interested in saving your marriage from a death by a thousand cuts, the plunge into these deeper waters will be worth it.

Special note to the reader:

Before we go any further, I want to make something clear. If you do not know the Lord as the Savior of your life, that is the first step you need to take. The Bible makes it clear that we cannot do anything without the Lord. It is only through His power that you will be able to implement the steps given throughout this guide. If you have not accepted Christ's free gift of salvation, I urge you to turn to the back of this book and find out what you've been missing. After that, feel free to read the rest of the book. Please don't skip this step. Your eternal life depends on it.

The real act of marriage takes place in the heart, not in the ballroom or church or synagogue. It's a choice you make--not just on your wedding day, but over and over again--and that choice is reflected in the way you treat your husband or wife.

Barbara
de Angelis

Chapter One:
The Golden Rule Amplified

You've heard of the Golden Rule, right? What about the Platinum Rule? The Golden Rule states, "Do unto others as you would have them do unto you." In contrast, the Platinum Rule says, "Treat others the way they want to be treated." Two different rules. Two different messages. So which one is right? Allow me to share a couple of scenarios, and then I'll answer that question.

Dean is enjoying his day off and spending some time on his hobbies. Around five in the evening, Janet calls to tell Dean that her boss called an emergency meeting, and she has no idea when she'll be home. After hanging up the phone, Dean wrestles with a decision. Since Janet didn't say anything about dinner, he could assume that he could fix himself some dinner and let her do the same. But Dean quickly realizes that if the roles were reversed, he would greatly appreciate if dinner was ready when he got home, so he rolls up his sleeves and gets busy in the kitchen.

David comes home from work with the news that he has been laid off. He is discouraged, depressed, and even though he doesn't want to admit it, he's scared. His wife, Paula, in an effort to encourage him, showers him with love and kisses. She reminds him of God's faithfulness through other trials and tries to help him see the positive side of things. Meanwhile, David becomes angry and frustrated, storms out the door and says, "I'll be back later." Paula is hurt and confused. What had she done wrong? After all, she was only treating David the way she would want to be treated if the roles had been reversed. Why did he get so angry?

In each of these scenarios, the Golden Rule was carried out. In the first scene, things worked out just as we would assume they should. Janet came home to a home-cooked meal, leaving her feeling relieved and loved. However, in the second scene, Paula's actions only led to more frustration for David. Why? Because David didn't need or want the kind of attention Paula was showering on him. Frankly, he just needed some time to be alone and think things over, but Paula didn't understand that. She wasn't thinking about the Platinum Rule.

So which rule is right? Actually, not only are they both right, but they are also both Scriptural. In fact, the conflict between the two rules has led to many Scriptural debates, but the truth is that the basis for both rules can be found in the Word of God. And as you can see from the two examples above, the key comes in understanding when to use each rule.

The Golden Rule can be found in Matthew 7:12 which says: *Therefore all things whatsoever ye would that men should do to you, do ye even so to them: for this is the law and the prophets.*

There are also several Biblical references to "love thy neighbor as thyself." When Jesus commanded us to do unto others as we would have them do unto us, He wasn't saying that *that* was as far as we should go. He was cautioning us to think about our actions and how we would feel if we were the recipient of those actions. If we did that, the world would certainly be a better, more peaceful place. But the message of the Bible doesn't stop there. The Golden Rule is a good start, but there's more. Philippians 2:3-4 continues the lesson: *Let nothing be done through strife or vainglory; but in lowliness of mind **let each esteem other better than themselves.** Look not every man on his own things, but every man also on the things of others.*

The Golden Rule focuses on what I want, but the Platinum rule follows this advice and goes beyond that. It encourages me not just to do what I want but to love the other person enough to find out how they want to be treated and act accordingly. It involves putting their wants and desires above my own.

Romans 12:10 concurs: *Be kindly affectioned one to another with brotherly love;* i**n honour preferring one another;** And so does I Corinthians 13:5, *[Charity] Doth not behave itself unseemly,* **seeketh not her own**, *is not easily provoked, thinketh no evil …*

So, you see, both rules are Biblical, and both are necessary if we are to live peaceably one with another. The question remains, how do we know which rule to use at any given time? The answer is fairly simple though I warn you, it is not easy. Get to know your loved one well enough that you'll know when they want to be treated the same way you want to be treated and when they prefer a different approach, and then act accordingly. When all else fails, remind yourself, "It's not about me!"

I teach the ladies' Sunday School class at my church, so every Sunday morning, I arrive early to set up for my lesson, and my precious husband, Jason, makes coffee for the ladies. What you must understand is that Jason likes his coffee STRONG. It has been known to get up and walk around all by itself. Okay, maybe not quite, but it is strong stuff!!!! And while some of our ladies enjoy it, most of them would rather have it weaker. So, my husband has adjusted his ratio of coffee to water. Instead of following the Golden Rule and making it the way he would want it to be made, he follows the Platinum Rule and makes it the way the ladies prefer it. And let me tell you, good coffee makes for a happy Sunday School hour!

Ladies, I'm sure you've already figured out by now that your husband doesn't think the same way you do. The truth is we're all different, and we all have different preferences when it comes to how we're treated. If you know that your man, like David in the scenario above, is prone to clam up when he's frustrated, then leave him alone. Don't try to make him talk about his problems. Sure, it may make you feel better, but will it help him? Not typically. If he needs time alone, give it to him. You'll both be better in the long run.

We hear so much about the Golden Rule, but it's a shame that more marriages aren't built on the Platinum Rule. If they were, they would probably last a lot longer. Allow me to boil it down for you. It's not about what you want. It's about giving your man what he wants. That's what love is all about! God demonstrated that when He sent His Son to die for us. Did He want to watch His Son suffer such agony on the cross? Absolutely not. But He did want to make a way for us to have what we want and what we so desperately need: a Savior.

God loves us enough to give. Let's follow the same example.

A great marriage is not when the "perfect couple" comes together. It is when an imperfect couple learns to enjoy their differences.

Dave Meurer

Chapter Two:

Just Do It!

Tyler offered to take over one of the house chores for Marcie to help lighten her load. Marcie gladly handed over the job of doing the dishes and wiping down the kitchen every evening. For the first few weeks, Tyler faithfully performed his cleaning and ensured that the kitchen was in good condition before he went to bed each night. Then, he started missing a night here and there, and pretty soon, he was missing more nights than he was doing. Marcie let it go, determined that since it was his job and he agreed to do it, she would make sure he did it, and she would not do it for him. But once the dishes started piling up, Marcie couldn't handle it anymore, and she took back over the chore of the dishes, complaining all the while that Tyler was not keeping up his end of the bargain.

Being the man of the house, Gus has the responsibility of the yard work, but lately, Gus has been finding other ways to spend his free time, and the yard has gotten out of control. Rhonda has mentioned the state of the yard on several occasions, but Gus only nods his head and says, "Yeah, I need to get around to it." After a couple of weeks, Rhonda is tired of reminding him, so in addition to her other chores, she takes on the role of "yard care specialist." But when Gus gets home from work, boy, does he get an earful about what Rhonda had to put up with to get the job done.

As we've already discussed, we all have jobs to do. Sometimes the jobs around the house are split evenly, and sometimes they're not, but that's not the point of this chapter. The point is our behavior and attitudes when our husbands don't follow through with things that they have promised to do, specifically referring to jobs around the house. I am not here to offer excuses for their failures to see things through, and believe me when I tell you that I have been exasperated myself when things weren't done in an orderly fashion. However, my attitude and reaction were just as wrong as my husband's inaction. You see, ladies, even if a particular task is not assigned to us, we can do it out of love instead of complaining about it not getting done. I mean, think about it, yes, we can try to make a point by saying, "It's his job and I'm not going to do it," but who does that really hurt in the long run? If we allow the job to go undone for days and then maybe weeks, aren't we the ones who suffer? Aren't we the ones who grow aggravated and bitter? If it was frustrating our husbands enough, they would do something about it, but obviously, it's not a big deal to them that it's not getting done. But it does bother us, so what's the solution?

Well, we could nag, which we know is neither right nor helpful, not to mention nurturing to our marriage. Or we could do the job ourselves out of love and respect for our spouse. After all, it takes as much time and energy to complain about the chore as it does to actually do it. And by doing the chore, at least we've spent the time and energy in a productive way. Besides, which approach do you think will build a happier, healthier home?

Let's take a look at Tyler and Marcie's situation. By not saying anything to Tyler about his failure to clean the kitchen, Marcie was creating a breeding ground for bitterness in her heart. Each time she saw the mess, her anger rose and her inner complaints began. She may have thought she was keeping the peace by not voicing her frustrations, but in the long run, she was creating a much bigger problem. That being said, Marcie's first reaction should have been to approach Tyler and kindly ask if there was a reason he wasn't completing his tasks in the kitchen. Who knows? He may have had a good excuse (sometimes our men do). If so, fine, let it go. If not, Marcie could have explained why it was important to her that Tyler keeps up with the chore he agreed to do. Most of the time, ladies, that's all it takes. If we tell our men that something is important to us, they'll usually try to make it happen. Not always, but usually.

The point is, we need to be patient, and if the chore is really bothering us that much, why not just do it? First Corinthians 13:4 reminds us, *Charity suffereth long, and is kind.* Did you catch that? Charity, which is another word for love, suffers a long time. In other words, it's patient. It's also kind. You know, kind, like doing a chore for someone else. Do it out of love. Do it for your own sanity. Do it because that's what Christ would do.

Remember the night of the Last Supper? Jesus and his twelve disciples were gathered together in the Upper Room to share a final meal together. But before sitting down at the table, Jesus, the King of Kings and

Lord of Lords, picked up a towel and a bowl of water and began washing the disciples' feet. Was that His job? Was that what He came to do? Shouldn't someone else have been responsible for such a lowly task? But Jesus was setting forth an example, and that lesson was this: love enough to take on the dirty jobs without a second thought. It doesn't make you weak; it makes you like Christ.

Rhonda (in scenario B) could certainly take this lesson to heart. Should Gus have done the yard work? Absolutely. Is there any excuse for his allowing things to get so far out of order? Probably not. But should that make Rhonda love him any less? Is that what love is all about? Is it based on performance? If so, we're all in trouble. No, love is a choice—a choice to accept and respect your husband in spite of his failings. So, he didn't keep up the yard work. Are we so perfect that we've never fallen behind on a task? Please note, I'm not excusing Gus's behavior, and I would advise Rhonda to follow the same advice as Marcie. That being said, I am trying to help you realize and remember that none of us is perfect. We all have faults and failures, and at times, we all fall short of what we've agreed to do. But don't allow your frustration over little things like dirty dishes and a few weeds to cause you to fall back on one of the biggest promises you've ever made. You know, the one that says, "For better or worse, in sickness and in health, till death do us part."

As the old saying goes, "Don't sweat the small stuff." Do what you need to do, but in all things, make sure love is in the center of it all. First John 3:18 says, *My little children, let us not love in word, neither in tongue; but in deed and in truth.* We can say that we love someone until we're blue in the face, but the fact of the matter is this: actions really do speak louder than words. So, I think it's about time we started acting as if we love our husbands. Let's do more than love in word; let's love in deed. Just do it!

Think not because you are wed,
that all your courtship's at an end.

Antonio Hurtado
de Mendoza

Chapter Three:
And the Award Goes To. . .

Sam gets home from work early and decides to empty the dishwasher. Typically, Sam would rather flop down on the couch and watch the ball game, but for some reason, he's struck with the idea of helping Beth out a bit with the housework. He knows she's been stressed lately, and he can't wait to see how happy she is when she finds out what he's done for her. However, when Beth comes home, she doesn't even mention the fact that the dishwasher has been emptied, and Sam gets angry.

Henry's job is to take the trash out on Tuesday evening, but for some reason, he can never seem to remember until Rachel reminds him. . .several times. One night, Henry actually remembers that the trash needs to go out and fulfills his task without being reminded, whistling all the while and anticipating the praise he'll receive from his wife, Rachel. But when she goes about her evening and doesn't acknowledge his assertiveness, Henry is annoyed.

All right, ladies, this is a tough one for us to understand. Typically, we are the "keepers at home," so not a day goes by when we don't complete a myriad of tasks around the house, usually in addition to our full-time jobs. We clean. We cook. We fold laundry. We sweep floors. We iron clothes. We do and do and do. Why? Because there are no such things as house cleaning fairies! Seriously, we do those things because they have to be done. We don't do them to get praise. For the most part, we don't do them in hopes that our husbands will notice and commend us for our hard work. We see what needs to be done on a daily basis, and we do it.

When was the last time your husband thanked you for the good meal you prepared or for having clean clothes to wear? When was the last time he applauded you for going to the grocery store (again!) or for balancing the checkbook (how do you balance negative numbers?)? Let's face, it doesn't typically happen, and you know what? We're okay with that. We don't expect it. Men, however, approach this whole "housework" topic with a different philosophy.

Whether the job they do is considered theirs or not, men desire praise and recognition from their wives. I don't know why, but it's true. Completing a simple task around the house gives them great pride in themselves (like they've climbed Mt. Everest or something), and they expect their wives to be just as proud of them. We, however, tend to overlook their "great accomplishments" because the tasks that they performed weren't all that "great" to us. They were typical, everyday chores that we've done a thousand times. What's the big deal? The big deal is that it's a big deal to our husbands, and that ought to be enough. So what if they don't acknowledge the housework we do? Is that really important? We need to put aside our selfishness, pride, bitterness, and the entire "it's not fair" attitude and give our men what they truly crave—respect and praise. Does it make what we've accomplished any less important?

We also need to understand that our husbands' motives for doing those "extra" things around the house differ from our motives. Why do we do the dishes or the laundry or the grocery shopping? Because they are all tasks that have to be done, right? So, in essence, our motive for doing housework is simply because it has to be done. That's it! But our precious men don't approach these tasks with the same motives. They don't do a chore because it has to be done. They do it to earn our love. Do they need to? No. We love them whether they help around the house or not, but let's be honest, ladies, don't we appreciate them that much more when they help out?

To Sam, emptying the dishwasher was a sign of love and appreciation for all the hard work that Beth does. To Beth, on the other hand, emptying the dishwasher was just another chore—a chore that she does all the time without thinking anything about it. Because of their different views and perspectives, Sam was hurt that his offer of love was taken for granted, and Beth was at a loss for words because she couldn't understand why it was such a big deal. If Beth would have stepped outside of her own world and limited viewpoint long enough to recognize what Sam meant by his action of emptying the dishwasher, perhaps her response would have been different.

As for Henry, well, he was doing a job that was already assigned to him, but by doing it without being prompted, he was trying to take some of the stress off of Rachel. Again, to Rachel, Henry was only doing his job, and for once, he was doing it without having to be reminded. While Rachel was appreciative of Henry's initiative, she did not understand his real motives behind doing what he did. And therefore, her lack of acknowledgment and praise was like a slap in the face to Henry.

Now, keep in mind, ladies, that when I say we need to appreciate and praise our husbands, I'm not talking about going overboard. I'm not talking about treating them like a dog. "Who's a good boy? Yes, that's my good boy." They're not stupid, nor are they lower lifeforms. They're just different, and a little praise from us goes a long way toward displaying our love and respect for them.

The last phrase in I Corinthians 8:1 tells us *charity edifieth*. In other words, love builds up others. It doesn't tear them down. Acknowledging your husband's "great accomplishments" (however small they may seem in your eyes) is an excellent way to build him up. Likewise, ignoring the things he does for you only tears him down. Do you love your man?

Then let him know it. Find something to praise him for each and every day and watch the love grow in his eyes. Pretty soon, he'll be looking for more and more ways to please you. How awesome would that be?

Love has nothing to do with what you are expecting to get--only with what you are expecting to give-- which is everything.

Katharine Hepburn

Chapter Four:

Check Your Expectations at the Door

John agrees to bring in firewood, but three hours later, the wood is still sitting by the back door, and the house is growing cooler by the moment. Not only is Amber frustrated by his procrastination, but she knows if she reminds him to bring in the wood, he'll accuse her of nagging him and proclaim that he heard her the first time. She also knows, however, that if she doesn't remind him, he'll forget about it, and the wood will still be sitting outside in the morning, long after the fire in the wood stove has gone out. Amber finds herself wishing that John were more like her and didn't procrastinate over necessary tasks.

It's Sunday morning, and once again, Paul is still in bed while Brittany is ironing clothes, fixing breakfast, and taking care of the kids. With just enough time to spare, Paul gets up, showers, dresses and eats breakfast. By the time they leave for church, Brittany feels exhausted, like she's already worked a full day while Paul feels fresh and ready for worship. On the drive to church, Brittany daydreams about a husband who would pay attention to the many needs outside of his own and be more willing to help out so that she didn't feel so frazzled every Sunday morning.

I don't think there's a woman alive who hasn't, at some point, wished that her husband were more like herself. On the one hand, we all know we have flaws —some of us more than others—and there are things about ourselves that we don't like and wouldn't want to have to put up with in our spouses.

On the other hand, there are areas of our lives that we feel we manage well and would like to see mirrored in our men. For example, as women, we tend to be better at multitasking and understanding what needs to be done, how long each task will take, and what order would be the most efficient to get everything accomplished. Most men seem to lack this particular skill and often fail to see beyond their own needs and obligations. It's not because they're lazy or uncaring but rather it's because that's what they're used to. In many ways, we have promoted that behavior.

We each have our own ways of doing things. Unfortunately, we tend to cling to those ways as the only right way when that is not, in fact, the case. In order to live in harmony with our husbands, we need to first realize that they are *not* us. They don't think like us. They don't act like us. They don't perform tasks in the same way that we do. And neither should we expect them to. As we have already discussed, they have different personalities and ways of doing things.

That doesn't make them wrong, only different.

One thing I want to make very clear is no matter how much our husbands' behavior irritates us, it is not our place to try to change them. We can talk to them and express our concerns about a particular behavior that we feel is impacting our relationships in a negative way. But we should never harp on them or degrade them in any way. For one thing, it's not loving. For another, that kind of treatment will only make them balk like stubborn mules. Rather than trying to change the way our men behave, how about trying to change our attitudes instead?

Ladies, our expectations will get us into trouble every time. Let's face it, we expect a lot out of life and those with whom we share it. We expect people to do things the way we think they should be done, and we expect things to turn out the way we want them to. Well, that's just not the way life works! The more we expect, the more we'll be disappointed. We would do well to tone down our expectations (even what we expect of ourselves), and approach life with more realistic hopes.

In scenario 1, Amber does have a predicament. On the one hand, if she says something about her husband's procrastination, he'll say she's nagging. On the other hand, if she doesn't say something, it's likely the job won't get done. In such cases, Amber needs to decide which end result is the least unpleasant and go for it. If the job is one that must be done and it truly looks like her husband is not going to complete the task, then she needs to be bold enough to remind him, but in a loving way. Remember, the Scripture encourages us to be sure our words are seasoned with grace, not venom. "John," she could say, "would you like me to help you bring in the wood?" This simple request could be the reminder he needed, and he'll get up and do it right away. If, however, he accuses her of nagging, she again needs to watch her words. "I'm sorry you feel that I'm nagging. That is not my intention. I only wanted to remind you in case you had forgotten." Yes, he may still grumble and complain, but you know what? That's how we all tend to respond when we're asked to stop doing the thing we want to do in order to do something we don't want to do. Give your husband the benefit of the doubt and also a reminder or two when needed.

As for Brittany in scenario 2, the best thing for her to do is to sit down and have a heart to heart with Paul. Obviously, Sunday morning, when she's already stressed, is NOT a good time for this discussion. Instead, she should plan to sit down with Paul one evening when they can have some uninterrupted quiet time to talk. With love and words seasoned with grace, she should explain how she's feeling, being careful to avoid accusatory words such as selfish or clueless. Who knows? Paul may be under the impression that trying to help Brittany would "throw off her groove." He may be trying to help by staying out of the way. The point is, neither Paul nor Brittany will understand the issue unless Brittany brings it up for discussion.

Proverbs 19:13 has some somber words about wives who complain when they're expectations aren't met. *The contentions of a wife are a continual dropping.* Contention. Strife. Anger. Complaints. It's like a continual dropping. This past year has been one of the wettest years I remember in my life, particularly this winter. It has rained and rained and rained. In fact, for nearly two straight weeks around Christmas, the sun never made an appearance. Despite the holiday spirit, the days were dark and dreary, and let me tell you, the constant downpour really began taking a toll on people's emotions. Endless rain will do that, and so will endless complaints. Be careful, ladies. I know we expect as much or more from ourselves as we do from our husbands, but often they are the ones who bear the brunt of our frustrations when those expectations aren't met.

In the words of Disney's Elsa, let it go!

Love recognizes no barriers.
It jumps hurdles, leaps fences,
penetrates walls to arrive at
its destination full of hope.

Maya
Angelou

Chapter Five:
Take a Hint

Ben comes home from work and finds Evelyn working in the kitchen, struggling to cook dinner, load the dishwasher, and help the kids with homework all at the same time. As soon as Ben enters the kitchen, Evelyn describes to him her tough and busy day, all the while juggling her other tasks. Ben, who has been leaning on the counter and watching as Evelyn talks, offers a brief apology for her troubles, then leaves the room and sits down in front of the television, leaving her to her one-woman circus.

Melissa hints around to Jeffrey about an upcoming concert she would like to attend. She even goes so far as to point out to her husband that the concert is the same day as her birthday. On the big day, Jeffrey surprises her with a birthday trip to the bowling alley. Melissa is less than pleased, and Jeffrey ought to be thankful that no one found his lifeless body in another kind of alley the next morning.

For many of us, we come home from full-time jobs only to work another full-time job of wife, mother, and homemaker. Guys have a tendency to forget this and sometimes don't understand how tiring it can be for us. They often come home from their full-time jobs and flop down on the couch or in front of the computer for some much-needed "down time." What they fail to realize is that we have no "down time." If we're not working at our jobs, we're working at home. And when we're not working at home, we're working at church.   While the men are enjoying their much-needed rest, we're preparing dinner, cleaning the house, getting a grocery list together, taking care of the kids and on and on and on.   Finally, after dinner is done, the kitchen is cleaned and the last of the laundry is folded and put away, we stumble to our bedrooms and collapse into a mindless stupor, only to rise and do it all again the next day.   We need help, and our husbands don't seem to get it.   Can we make it any more obvious? Actually, yes, we can.

We need to understand that guys have a unique form of communication. They are blunt and to the point, almost to a fault. They say what they mean and mean what they say. Because of this form of communication, men don't understand "women talk," which consists of many levels of emotion, subtlety, and words.

For example, when Evelyn described her bad day, all Ben heard was that his wife was in a bad mood. What he didn't realize was that she was crying out for help. Instead of being frustrated by Ben's seeming lack of concern, Evelyn needed to realize that she was speaking "chick chat." She was saying what she wanted and needed without really saying what she wanted or needed. Let's face it, ladies, men don't get subtlety, and they don't understand hints. Get this through your head now, and it will save you a lot of frustration in the future. If Evelyn wanted help, she should have directly asked for help. "Ben, could you help the kids with their homework while I finish up dinner?" Or maybe, "Ben, I could use some help here in the kitchen. Would you rather fix dinner or load the dishwasher?" Simple. Direct. To the point.

At times like this, we could learn a lot from the story of Martha in the Bible. Remember Martha? She invited Jesus and his followers into her home for dinner without realizing that her sister was going to leave her to do all the work. I have no doubt that, throughout the evening, Martha gave Mary several signals that she wanted help. Perhaps a roll of the eyes or a tilt of the head. Maybe she even gave her sister the evil eye or cleared her throat in such a way that everyone looked up. Everyone except Mary, that is. It seems she only had eyes for Jesus.

In a fit of frustration and fatigue, Martha finally lost it, but instead of directly asking Mary for help, she accused Jesus of playing favorites. *But Martha was cumbered about much serving, and came to him, and said, Lord, dost thou not care that my sister hath left me to serve alone? bid her therefore that she help me.- Luke 10:40* I wonder if the story would have turned out differently if Martha had simply asked for help to begin with.   And think about it, she was speaking Mary's language—girl talk.   This wasn't wife-to-husband conversation, it was between two sisters. So, if Mary, being a woman herself, didn't understand Martha's needs, how can we expect our husbands to understand our needs unless we tell them?

Now, how about poor Melissa in the second scenario I set forth at the beginning of the chapter? I mean, to us ladies, Jeffrey seems like an insensitive jerk. Good grief, Melissa just about drew him a picture. She told him about the concert. She expressed interest in going to the concert. She pointed out that the concert was on her birthday. Get a clue, man!!!!! But, interestingly enough, for all that she said and did, Melissa neglected to ask Jeffrey if he would take her to the concert. Sure, she may have been hoping not to spell it out so that there was some surprise in it for her, but her failure to be direct left her with a surprise she wasn't pleased with.

What Melissa failed to realize was that Jeffrey's gift to the bowling alley was actually very thoughtful. Knowing how much Melissa enjoyed bowling, he regretted that she didn't have the time to do such things anymore and wanted to provide her with an evening to relax and do one of her favorite things. What seemed to Melissa to be unthoughtful and uncaring was actually a very romantic gesture. Only Melissa didn't see it that way because she expected him to understand her hints and suggestions about the concert.

If we want or need something, we need to be direct and to the point. Don't nag or whine or complain. State our needs in a clear, concise way that cannot be misunderstood, and more often than not, our men will be happy to comply.

Just so you don't think I'm being hard on our hubbies or men in general, here's Biblical proof that men don't get hints and subtlety. Jesus, as you know, taught in parables (earthly stories with heavenly meanings). He did this to help the people understand what he was saying which is a classic teaching method. To help students understand something that is foreign to them, equate it with something that is familiar. As the greatest Teacher that has ever walked the earth, Jesus utilized this method of getting His message across. Unfortunately, his disciples didn't always get it. In fact, on one occasion, they even said to Him: *Lo, now speakest thou plainly, and speakest no proverb. (John 16:29)* If the Son of God couldn't get a group of men to understand without being direct and to the point, why should we think we can? Again, I'm not being hard on men. They're just wired with a different form of communication, and if we want to live peaceably with them, it's time we start communicating with them in their own language.

Love me when I least deserve it
because that's when I really need it.

Swedish
proverb

Chapter Six:

The Unspoken Compliment

In an effort to please and surprise her husband, Michelle spends the entire day cleaning the house from top to bottom. She goes so far as to wash the curtains and dust the crown molding. At the end of the day, Michelle is exhausted but thrilled with the results of her hard work. She eagerly anticipates Tony's reaction to the clean state of their home, but when Tony gets home, he doesn't seem to notice that anything is different. He doesn't look around. He doesn't compliment her hard work. In just a few minutes, Michelle goes from feeling ecstatic to feeling angry and frustrated. How could Tony not have noticed and appreciated all that she had done?

While preparing herself for her date night with her husband, Laura decides to go all out. She spends extra time on her hair and applies more makeup than usual—all in an attempt to make herself beautiful and alluring in Lee's eyes. She exits the bedroom with a spring in her step, but the spring soon loses its bounce when all Lee can say is "I thought you'd never be ready to go." He seems totally oblivious to the fact that Laura has spent extra time and effort to look nice for him. His lack of attention and praise causes Laura to go on her date feeling hurt and unloved.

I'm sure we've all had events similar to those above happen in our own lives. We go out of our way to do something special—perhaps preparing an elaborate meal or planning a unique event—and our efforts seem as if they're completely in vain. Our men, bless their hearts, don't intend to hurt our feelings, but we can't imagine that they could have missed the time and effort involved in what we've done for them.

When we put time and effort into something, we expect our men to notice. Is that too much to ask? The task was a big deal to us, so we assume that it will be a big deal to them. After all, remember, men like to receive praise and acknowledgment for their accomplishments, so why should we be any different? This is where that Golden Rule principle comes back into play. We would think that they would treat us the same way they would want to be treated. If they had spent all day on a task, they would want us to notice and praise them for it, right? But there seems to be a disconnect when the roles are reversed.

As for us, remember that we have issues with setting expectations. When we don't get the reaction we are hoping for, we feel slighted, disappointed, and even angry. What we fail to take into consideration, however, is that even though our husbands often fail to take notice of our efforts and achievements, they don't usually take note of our lack of achievement either.

No, Tony didn't say anything to Michelle about how nice the house looked, but he has never said anything negative about her housekeeping skills when the house was a mess either.   For the entire winter, while Michelle was busy with projects outside the home, the house was a disaster.   Stacks and piles of mail and other material littered every surface in the home.   Dust bunnies took over the flooring.   The bathrooms began to resemble war zones. And on more than one occasion, the family had to eat out because there was no food or clean dishes in the house.

I can hear some of you arguing, "Well, Tony should have helped out more, and things wouldn't have gotten so bad." Yes, that's true. The entire running of the household should not be left up to Michelle; however, that is not the point here. The point is that, during that entire winter, Tony could have complained about the disarray. He could have murmured when he didn't have clean clothes to wear to work. But, just as he didn't seem to notice the immaculate state of the home after Michelle cleaned, neither did he seem to notice the growing chaos when she didn't clean—either that or it truly didn't bother him. The point is that while he wasn't applauding Michelle's hard work, neither was he critical of her lack of housework in previous days. Keeping that in mind, I'm sure, would have helped Michelle in this instance.

Now, let's talk about Lee. Yes, he should have noticed and appreciated the fact that Laura dressed up for him, but in Lee's eyes, Laura is beautiful whether she's dressed up or in her pajamas with her hair a mess and wearing no makeup. How many times had he come up to her first thing in the morning when Laura was fresh out of bed and whispered in her ear, "Good morning, beautiful"? How many times had he caught her when she felt she looked her absolute worst, looked her in the eye and said, "You're so gorgeous"?

Lee's response that night was a compliment, not an insult. When Laura looked in the mirror, she saw something different. She saw the results of hard work, and after all that effort, she felt prettier. Perhaps Lee didn't notice the "fix up" because to him, Laura is always lovely. Does that mean Laura shouldn't have bothered? No, not at all. If dressing up a little extra made Laura feel better about herself, then it was definitely worth it whether Lee said anything about it or not.

Ladies, instead of focusing on all the times our men don't say what we want them to say, let's try focusing on all the times they don't say anything negative—especially those times when it would be appropriate and well-deserved. Let's take their silence as an unspoken compliment, and leave it at that.

First Peter 4:8 tells us, *And above all things have fervent charity among yourselves: for charity shall cover the multitude of sins.* Are you allowing your love for your husband to cover his mistakes?

Love overlooks faults and forgives when mistakes are made. Keep that in mind the next time your husband fails to offer a compliment.

I love you not only for what you are,
but for what I am when I am with you.
I love you not only for what you have
made of yourself, but for what
you are making of me.

Roy
Croft

Chapter Seven:

Mr. Fixit

Sandy comes home from work, frustrated about some of her fellow employees and how their behavior is affecting the quality of her own work. For fifteen minutes straight, Sandy vents her feelings of frustration, all the while trying to sort out how to deal with the myriad of emotions that are all fighting for her attention. When she finally takes a breath, her husband, Bryce, begins to speak—only his words are not those of sympathy or encouragement. Instead,

Bryce lays out a step-by-step plan for Sandy to follow to improve her efficiency at work and deal with her fellow employees.

Tabitha expresses to Charles that she's feeling overwhelmed with her many responsibilities. Between her full-time job, chores at home, family time, church obligations, and everything else on her plate, Tabitha is quickly growing weary in well doing. She longs for Charles to hold her and tell her that everything is going to be okay. She even goes so far as to hope that her cry for help will resonate with Charles in such a way that perhaps he'll offer to take on some of the chores around the house. (Maybe she needs to read the chapter, *Take a Hint.*) Instead, Charles lectures her on how she takes on too many tasks and tries to dictate a schedule to help her get more done in less time.

Ladies, I have a startling announcement. Most guys don't want to encourage us as much as they want to solve our problems. It's not that they're being cruel, unkind, or unloving. It is simply that, by nature, men are problem solvers. If we state a problem, they automatically assume that we want them to fix it. That's not what we want at all, at least, not typically. As women, we tend to share and voice our problems because it helps us sort things out. Often, by the time we've finished venting, we already see the solution to the problem. We just had to get it out in the open. We needed to talk it through with someone, and for some reason, we felt that our husbands were the prime candidates. Unfortunately, they don't understand our need to vent because men only share their problems when they're hoping for a solution. It's simply their way of thinking. It's the way God made them. So, how can we convey our feelings to our men without them donning their "Mr. Fixit" uniform?

First off, we need to understand the problem-solving nature of men and not get offended when their first reaction is to fix rather than to encourage. Our first reaction is to share the problem, right? And we do this even when we know that our men are not going to respond in the way we want them to, so you would think we would be prepared for their gut reactions.

Secondly, if encouragement or a listening ear is all we want, we need to tell our husbands that before we begin our venting session. Something simple like, "I'm not looking for solutions. I just need to get these feelings out in the open. Could you please just listen for a little bit?" While, in the back of their minds, the wheels will still be turning trying to figure out how to fix your problem, your husband will also take into consideration your request and try to keep his problem solving to himself. That's not to say that he will always be successful, but in the long run, you may also find that his problem-solving methods are not only appropriate but also effective. And you'll be happy that you allowed him to express his gift and insight.

Thirdly, and some of you may not like this, but it is the truth and it must be said. We need to talk it out with the Father first. If all we want is to get it out in the open and work things out, who better to tell than our loving Heavenly Father? Unlike our husbands, He understands what we're feeling and what we're trying to accomplish through our "venting session." He will listen to our cries for as long as we need, and oftentimes, He will speak to us in that still, small voice. He will whisper peace to our souls and often give us a verse of guidance or encouragement. After that, we may or may not want or need to rehearse the event to our husbands. Plus, they won't have to listen to us complain. It's a win-win situation.

Heaviness in the heart of man maketh it stoop: but a good word maketh it glad. - Proverbs 12:25

*If you would like to see a humorous depiction of this topic, visit YouTube and search for the video, "It's Not About the Nail." It's hilarious!

What greater thing is there for two human souls than to feel that they are joined for life--to strengthen each other in all labor, to rest on each other in all sorrow, to minister to each other in silent, unspeakable memories at the moment of the last parting?

George
Eliot

What Happened to Prince Charming?

Chapter Eight:

Let's Talk

Isaac has been finding more and more reasons to miss church. Faith is concerned how his behavior is affecting the family, especially their teenage boy. Faith knows that Isaac is supposed to be the spiritual head of the home, but she fears if she says anything about him falling short in that area, he'll get angry with her.

Vivian works from home, and even though she and Steve have an understanding that it is the responsibility of both of them to raise their children, Steve often comes home and does his own thing while Vivian helps the kids with homework, science fair projects, and the making of baked goods for the school fundraiser. Steve's behavior has become a habit, and Vivian is beginning to feel as if Steve doesn't understand how demanding her job is and how much she needs help in raising the kids and keeping the house in order. As frustrated as she is, though, she is afraid to voice her feelings for fear of starting a long, drawn-out argument.

Fear of our husbands' reactions often keeps us from saying things that need to be said. When we bottle up all those negative feelings and emotions, we begin to grow bitter. Imagine putting a glass of spoiled milk on the counter. Each time you feel frustrated, you add to that glass. As if it weren't bad enough when you started, the milk will grow more rancid each time you add more to it, and for every day you allow it to linger, it will eventually overflow the glass.

Even if our confession of frustration leads to an argument, it's best to get our issues out in the open before they have time to grow into bitterness and resentment. Here are a few tips for successful conversation:

1) Mind your approach. When bringing a subject to your husband's attention, don't start with an accusation. That is a surefire way to lead to an argument. Instead, begin by asking your spouse if it is a good time to discuss a situation that has been heavy on your heart. From there, ask him about his thoughts or feelings on the subject you wish to discuss. This will give you a good idea where he's coming from so that you will better know how to broach the subject. Once you understand his thoughts and feelings, if there is still an issue, ask him to hear you out and to let you fully explain your feelings and concerns before he says anything. Again, be careful to avoid the "blame game" and instead only state the facts and your feelings based on those facts.

2) Mind your tone. Whatever you do, don't talk down to your husband or raise your voice to him. If you want him to listen to you and respect what you have to say, then say it in a way that is respectful to him. Many times the delivery of any speech is more about the tone than the actual words that are spoken. Keep this in mind throughout the conversation no matter how emotional you may feel.

3) Mind your attitude. This is the main reason that it is important to deal with issues before they have a chance to grow and fester into bitterness and resentment. The longer that they have been going through your mind and the more that you have rehearsed the hurt, the more attitude you're likely to have when you finally take the chance to get everything out in the open. When it is your turn to speak, before you open your mouth, think about the words that you're about to say, and ask yourself, "Are these words of love?" and "Am I seeking resolution with these words, or am I simply using them as an

outlet for my pain?" If the words need to be said, then say them. But again, watch your tone, and keep your attitude in check. The better you follow these three rules, the more likely it is that you'll have a successful and productive conversation in dealing with the issues that are causing you grief.

Ephesians 4:29 reminds us, *Let no corrupt communication proceed out of your mouth, but that which is good to the use of edifying, that it may minister grace unto the hearers.* In other words, every word out of our mouth ought to be used to lift others up, not tear them down. That's not to say that we'll never need to communicate about negative issues, but when we do, we must make sure that we speak the truth in love (Ephesians 4:15) and season our words with grace (Colossians 4:6). This applies to everyone with whom we speak, but especially our husbands!

After approaching Isaac and settling on a good time for their conversation, Faith could begin by asking her husband, "What does it mean to you to be the spiritual head of the home?" Isaac obviously knows that missing church is wrong, but perhaps he hasn't thought about how his behavior is affecting the rest of the family. After Isaac answers, Faith could continue by stating her concerns: "I fear that Timothy [their son] is having a hard time dealing with you not going to church, and I'm not sure what to tell him." From there, the conversation will begin to unfold, and if Faith will mind her tone and attitude, she may get to the root of the problem and possibly even the solution.

As for Vivian, she has every reason to be upset by Steve's behavior, especially if they have already discussed the need for both of them to be involved in the rearing of their children. If she's afraid that broaching the subject will lead to a long argument, then she needs to plan accordingly and only bring up the topic when they have plenty of uninterrupted time to talk. The conversation could begin like this, "Steve, I don't know if you've noticed, but I've been feeling very overwhelmed lately. I have a lot on my plate, and

I could really use your help with the kids." Once again, that single statement may be all that needs to be said for Steve to realize that he's been neglecting his share of the work. Or perhaps he's had something on his mind, and Vivian's courage to broach the subject opens the door for Steve to spill out his feelings about his current frustrations. It may sound strange to us, but sometimes men hide their pain by losing themselves in things they enjoy such as sports, television, video games, and so on. By doing things they enjoy doing, they are able to take their minds off their pressing problems.

Simply put, ladies, let's give our husbands a little slack. No, they're not perfect, but last time I checked, neither are we. Besides, sometimes their behavior may be their way of masking more serious problems that they're hesitant to discuss. Our willingness to communicate with them about the difficult things might be just the thing they need to get their problems out in the open and their bottoms off the couch!

Love does not consist of gazing at each other, but in looking outward together in the same direction.

Antoine de
Saint Exupery

Chapter Nine:
Do What Works

William is doing projects around the home and has asked Heather to pitch in. Heather despises helping William with tasks around the house because it always leads to an argument. William wants things done a certain way, but instead of explaining that to Heather, he expects her to know and understand what he wants. When Heather can't comply, William grows aggravated and says things he doesn't mean which leads Heather to grow frustrated and say things she doesn't mean. In the end, they're both mad, and the project is still incomplete.

Jose and Stacey are off for their yearly camping trip. Jose is looking forward to the vacation, but, as much as Stacey enjoys time with the family, she is dreading the trip. For Jose, camping means spending time with the kids, walking trails, fishing, and doing all the fun outdoor activities. For Stacey, however, it means staying by the camp, cooking all the food, cleaning up the dishes, taking care of everyone's needs. In short, what is a vacation for Jose is basically just another work week for Stacey, only without the conveniences of home.

While it is important for husbands and wives to spend time together and do things together, it is also imperative to understand that not every project needs to be done together, and some projects are best done separately. In other words, if you know a project or activity will bring one or both of you strife, then it's probably best to avoid doing it together, if at all possible. For a while, my husband and I tried to share the after-dinner cleanup, but we quickly discovered that the chore was best done by one of us, not both. I had one order of doing things; my husband had another.   I loaded the dishes into the dishwasher a certain way; my husband loaded them another. I had a particular method and cleaner for wiping down the counters; my husband's way differed. All in all, we only succeeded in getting in each other's way and on each other's nerves. Realizing this was the case, we made a new plan: he would clean the kitchen while I folded and put away laundry. This works wonderfully, and we're both much happier because of it. Plus, two chores are getting done in the same amount of time as we were previously accomplishing only one.

Romans 12:18 says, *If it be possible, as much as lieth in you, live peaceably with all men.* For some couples, that means working together on just about every task. For others, it means having some apart time and finding things that they can do together peaceably.

For William and Heather, it would be best for William to have someone else help him with the household repairs, preferably someone who understands William's working method. Not only would this leave Heather free to work on a different task, but it would prevent a lot of strife and hard feelings. If William does ask Heather to help, she can kindly explain her reasons for not wanting to get involved in the process and suggest that he call a friend to help. William may not understand to begin with, but in the end, he'll be glad he took his wife's advice.

For Jose and Stacey, it's good that they want to get away and have time together, but obviously, there is a miscommunication on one or both parts as to whether or not Stacey feels that camping really qualifies as a vacation. If the activity causes undue stress or strain on the relationship, it would probably be best for the two of them to decide on a better vacation idea or, at the very least, share the workload while on the camping trip. It is up to Stacey to point this out to Jose rather than expecting him to figure it out on his own.   After all, he's not the one who is unhappy with the current arrangements.

Hear me, and hear me well, couples do not need to do *everything* together. In fact, it's healthy for couples to have some alone time. Time to get away from each other. Time where they can sort out their feelings. Time to meet their own needs so that they can better meet the needs of their spouse.

That being said, it is also healthy for the relationship to find hobbies and activities that you can both enjoy together.   It doesn't have to be anything extravagant or costly, but something that the two of you can share.   For my husband and me, one of those things is hiking, as I discussed earlier.   For us, hiking is a time for us to come apart from everything and everyone else (except for our dog, Mitch, who would be crushed if we left him behind). It's just us in the quiet of nature. No televisions. No cell phones because reception is usually poor. No computers or tablets. And best of all, no interruptions. It is a place where we can talk or not, depending on our moods. We often share dreams, create stories and genuinely enjoy one another's company. It is on the trail, away from the rest of the world, that we feel closest.

I encourage you to find a passion that you and your husband can share. You'll be amazed at how close you'll feel to one another when you can work together on a task or activity that you both enjoy. Try it and see!

A successful marriage requires
falling in love many times,
always with the same person.

Mignon
McLaughlin

Chapter Ten:
Whatever!

Vanessa is trying to decide what to get everyone on her Christmas list. When she approaches her husband, Cameron, about what to get his parents, his frustrating response to her is "Well, since you're buying the gifts, whatever you think is fine with me." Vanessa is frustrated beyond belief that Cameron won't even take a few minutes to discuss the options with her, especially since she's the one that has to go out and do all the shopping, not to mention the wrapping.

In the midst of her crazy morning schedule, Tracey is trying to decide what to have for dinner so she can make any necessary plans to defrost the meat or stop by the store on her way home. When Parker enters the room, Tracey offers him two dinner options to choose from, to which he replies, "It doesn't matter. Either one is fine." Tracey is frustrated that, once again, all the decisions are left in her lap. She feels that it only adds to her daily stress.

Let's face it, gals, there are three phrases that make us cringe and cause our blood pressure to shoot through the roof. Those three phrases are *Whatever, I don't care,* and *It doesn't matter.* To us, each of these phrases is simply a way to shift the responsibility back in our laps, and typically, the annoying phrase is uttered while our husbands are doing their own things, not even bothering to look up when they respond. How rude!

I have left this topic for last because it is one of the most frustrating, and, therefore, the most difficult problems to solve in the husband-wife relationship. In no way is it acceptable for our men to shift the responsibility to us and expect us to make all the decisions regarding the running of the household. However, I must point out that, once again, we have been part of the problem rather than the solution. By asserting our desires so often above our husbands' wishes or pitching fits to have our way, is it any wonder our husbands have retreated and chosen the path of least resistance, which is to basically say, "Whatever you want, honey, is fine with me"? We have, in essence, created our monsters, and now, even when we want an answer or honest opinion, we can't get one. So what do we do?

First off, when asking your husband an important question, make sure it is a good time for him to answer. Firing questions at him as he's walking out the door for work is not likely to yield good results.

Next, be sure you have his undivided attention before asking him anything. Remember, men are not multi-taskers. If your man is doing something else, he is not listening to you. He can't do both. Then, once you have his attention, make your questions direct and to the point, filling in as much information as is necessary without adding in details that are insignificant to the conversation. Men like "man details" which means the smallest amount of information they need to know. For example, if a friend calls and tells you that a mutual friend is in the hospital with chest pains, then that's all your husband wants to know. He doesn't want to know how the chest pains came about, when they came about, what kind of medication the friend is on, what the doctors are saying is the possible cause, etc. Right now, to him, the only pertinent information is that the friend is in the hospital. Keep that in mind when asking your questions.

If, after that, he still won't give you an actual answer, explain to him how important it is to have his participation in the making of decisions and how stressful it is for you to feel as if you have to make all the decisions for everyone in the household. He may think that the answers of *Whatever* or *It doesn't matter* are his way of being easy going and may not understand how frustrating those answers are to you. This is your opportunity to set him straight, not in a vengeful way, but in a loving and productive way. For example, you could say something like, "Thank you for trying to be easy to please. I really do appreciate that, but in the future, it would actually be more helpful to me if you could give me a direct answer. Could you do that for me?" Chances are, he will be willing to do that though that's not to say that he'll always remember. He'll slip back into his bad habits just as we do, so he'll need your help.

First Corinthians 13:5 covers this topic in so many ways. *[Charity]Doth not behave itself unseemly, seeketh not her own, is not easily provoked, thinketh no evil;* Love doesn't behave itself unseemly, like pitching a fit when we have to make one more decision during the day. Is it really that big a deal? Or how about the fact that love seeketh not her own? In other words, love makes it about the other person, not about ourselves. It's not selfish. Love is also not easily provoked, so what does that say about us when we get all out of sorts over a simple decision? Unfortunately, it says we're not loving the way we should. And lastly, love doesn't think evil. No negative thoughts about how uncooperative our hubbies are being. No gripes and complaints about how helpless and hopeless they are. Love doesn't allow frustrations to overshadow it. Love is love, for better or worse.

So, let me ask you, how's your love for your husband? Is it still burning hot? If not, why not? Don't be too quick to cast the blame at him. Remember, love is a choice—a choice we must all make day after day, through the good times and the bad. Our marriages will be what we make of them. The choice is ours.

Duty gets offended quickly if it isn't appreciated, but love learns to laugh a lot and to work for the sheer joy of doing it. Obligation can pour a glass of milk, but quite often, love adds a little chocolate.

Linda Andersen

Conclusion:

Is That It?

I know this book has been brief, but I assure you, that was the point. I know you're busy, and I know you're tired. The last thing you need is a 200-page book on how to make your life easier and less stressful. Who has time for that? So, I hope that in these brief chapters you have found some answers for which you have been searching.

As for the ultimate question—What happened to Prince Charming—well, the answer is simple. He has grown and changed in response to how the world around him has changed, just as you have. No, he may not seem like the same man you married, and truth be told, he's not. But that doesn't have to be a bad thing. Change can be good, but a lot of it depends on how we choose to view it.

No one ever said that "happily ever after" would be easy. It isn't. But it is possible if we will only be willing to accept the fact that life brings about changes, and it is how we respond to those changes that determines whether we'll live happily ever after or not. It will take work and determination on our part, but our marriages are worth it, right?

Above all things, keep in mind that this is not something you have to accomplish on your own. In fact, as I stated before, you can't do it on your own. But with God, all things are possible. Cling to Him. Seek His advice. Walk in His love. And allow Him to mold you into the adoring wife you've always wanted to be.

If you take only one thing away from this book, let it be this. Philippians 4:8 says, *Finally, brethren, whatsoever things are true, whatsoever things are honest, whatsoever things are just, whatsoever things are pure, whatsoever things are lovely, whatsoever things are of good report; if there be any virtue, and if there be any praise, think on these things.* This verse contains excellent advice for all areas of our lives, our marriages included.

When thinking of our husbands, let us filter our thoughts according to this standard. Are these thoughts true? Are they honest? Are they just? Pure? Lovely? And lastly, are they of good report? If we can't answer "yes" to every one of those questions, then those thoughts need to be stopped in their tracks, for they will only lead to heartache and frustration. As II Corinthians 10:5 instructs us, let us bring every thought into captivity in obedience to the Lord, and instead of looking for the faults of our husbands, let us look for their strengths. Let's focus on the good things instead of the bad.   That alone will improve our relationships and increase our desire to be with and to please our husbands.

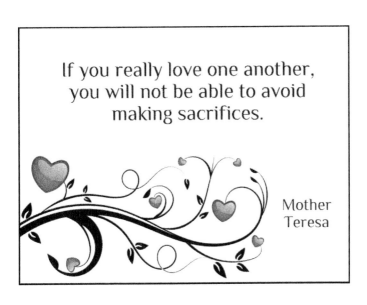

If you really love one another,
you will not be able to avoid
making sacrifices.

Mother
Teresa

The Plan of Salvation

Who hath prevented me, that I should repay him?
whatsoever is under the whole heaven is mine. - Job
41:11

God is speaking in this passage. In fact, He had been speaking for a few of the previous chapters. Reading through it, you'll notice that God is attempting to set a few things straight for Job and his "friends" (yes, I use that word loosely). In a nutshell, God asked, "Who do you think you are? Were you here when I created the world? Do you understand how the universe works? Are you all-powerful? No, I didn't think so. So what gives you the right to question me?" OUCH! (There's quite a lesson in there for all of us, huh?)

Interestingly enough, in the midst of that theme, we find Job 41:11 in which God basically states, "I don't owe anyone anything!" Point made. . . or is it? Funny, I think we would all agree with that statement. We nod and state in absolutes that God does not owe us a thing. Yet, is that how we act? Don't we expect His blessings? Don't we expect Him to answer our prayers? Don't we expect Him to give us strength to face the day?

"Well, sure," you may say, "but God has promised us those things, and that's the only reason we expect them."

Okay, I'll give you that, but what about expecting things that He hasn't promised. For example, how many times (like Job and his friends) have we demanded explanations from God for our current circumstances? How often have we demanded our way? On how many occasions have we grown angry with God because He didn't live up to our expectations and meet our needs in the way we saw fit? Our lips may say that we understand that God doesn't owe us anything, but our lives often tell a different story.

While I'm not, by any means, justifying our entitlement issues, may I offer the suggestion that maybe we expect more from God because we understand His giving nature? After all, God didn't owe us anything. In fact, we owed Him. But that didn't prevent John 3:16: *For God so loved the world, that he gave his only begotten Son, that whosoever believeth in him should not perish, but have everlasting life.*

God gave. Not because it was owed. Not because it was expected. But rather because we were loved. In order to display His great love for us, He gave it all—His only begotten Son. I don't know that we'll ever understand the full importance and impact of that sacrifice. To pay such a great price knowing that many would not accept the gift. To suffer such anguish and grief knowing that some would mock His name and scorn His sacrifice. To give so much for a population that was not worth such a price. No, God did not owe us a thing, but still He gave. Aren't you glad He did?

Perhaps you've heard about this great sacrifice but have not yet accepted the gift of salvation. If so, I urge you to call on His name today. Accept the free gift of salvation. Receive Him as Jesus your Lord. If you need help, please contact me through my website, DanaRongione.com. I would love to show you the way!

The fact of the matter is this: we are living in the last days. Jesus' return is imminent, and if you have not accepted His payment for your sins, you will be left behind to endure tribulation like this world has never known. I don't want that to happen to you, and neither does God. He's offered a way of escape. He's paid the ultimate price. All you have to do is accept it. Will you do it today? Remember, God doesn't owe anyone anything, which means you may not have another day or even another breath. This is the hour. Don't wait any longer. Receive the free gift that was offered out of love.

In the eyes of God, you were worth dying for!

God never intended for salvation to be difficult.

In fact, He made it as simple as A-B-C!

Admit: Admit that you are a sinner. A sinner is anyone who has done anything wrong at anytime. A lie, a bad attitude, a negative thought, pride—all of these things (and more) are sins. We are all guilty and deserve the ultimate penalty for sin: death.

For all have sinned and come short of the glory of God. - Romans 3:23

Believe: Believe that Jesus Christ is the Son of God, who came willingly to die on the cross to pay the debt for our sins and then rose again to return to Heaven, awaiting the day God will call all His children home to live with Him for all eternity. Because of His sacrifice, we can have eternal life.

For God so loved the world, that he gave his only begotten Son, that whosoever believeth in him should not perish, but have everlasting life. - John 3:16

Confess: Confess that Jesus is Lord of your life. The Bible tells us that even the devils believe and tremble. Belief is a vital step, but you must put that faith into action by surrendering your life and your will into His hands. Give Him control of everything you have and everything you are.

That if thou shalt confess with thy mouth the Lord Jesus, and shalt believe in thine heart that God hath raised him from the dead, thou shalt be saved. - Romans 10:9

About the Author

Dana Rongione is a Christian author and speaker living in Greenville, SC with her husband, Jason, and her spoiled dog, Mitchell.

For a living, she writes quality Christian books for audiences of all ages and speaks to women on a variety of inspirational and encouraging topics. For fun, Dana devours more books than she does chocolate (though not by much). She also enjoys hiking, playing the piano, and spending time with her family. To find out more about Dana and her ministry, visit her website at www.DanaRongione.com.

Books/Products by Dana Rongione

Adult Devotional/Christian Living:

He's Still Working Miracles: Daring To Ask God for the Impossible

There's a Verse for That

'Paws'itively Divine: Devotions for Dog Lovers

The Deadly Darts of the Devil

What Happened To Prince Charming? - Ten Tips To Achieve a Happy Marriage Life and Live Happily Ever After

Giggles and Grace Series:

Random Ramblings of a Raving Redhead

Daily Discussions of a Doubting Disciple

Lilting Laments of a Looney Lass

Mindful Musings of a Moody Motivator

Other Titles for Adults:

Improve Your Health Naturally

Creating a World of Your Own: Your Guide to
    Writing Fiction

The Delaware Detectives Mystery Series:

Book #1 – The Delaware Detectives: A Middle-
Grade Mystery

Book #2 – Through Many Dangers

Book #3 – My Fears Relieved

Book #4 - I Once Was Lost

Books for Young Children:

Through the Eyes of a Child

God Can Use My Differences

Audio:

Moodswing Mania – a study through select Psalms (6 CD's)

The Names of God – a 6-CD set exploring some of the most powerful names of God

Old Testament Miracles – a 4-CD set of in-depth study on OT Miracles

There's a Verse for That – Scripture with a soft music background

If you enjoyed this book, please consider leaving a review. You can help spread the word about my ministry of hope and encouragement. Thank you!

How would you like to have devotions delivered to your inbox every weekday? It's simple! Go to www.danarongione.com and sign up for my daily devotions, *A Word Fitly Spoken*. Don't worry—it's free!

Printed in Great Britain
by Amazon